Charismatic Leadership
A How to Guide

David Tuffley

To my beloved Nation of Four
Concordia Domi – Foris Pax

Charisma is the result of effective leadership, not the other way around — Warren Bennis & Burt Nanus [1].

Published 2012 by Altiora Publications
AltioraPublications.com/
ISBN-13: 978-1469994482, ISBN-10: 1469994488

About the Author
David Tuffley PhD is a lecturer in the School of ICT at Griffith University in Australia. The content of this book is the product of research performed while an employee of Griffith University, principally in relation to his work on the nature and practice of leadership.

Acknowledgements
Special thanks are due to my partner Angela for her unwavering support and encouragement.

Contents

INTRODUCTION 1

CHAPTER 1: THE NATURE OF CHARISMA 2

CHAPTER 2: CHARISMA & SELF-ACTUALIZATION 8

CHARACTERISTICS OF SELF-ACTUALIZED PEOPLE...............9
EXPERIENCE LIFE WHOLEHEARTEDLY, NOW 9
YOUR PRIMARY REALITY IS A RICH INNER LIFE................11
HONESTY WITH ONESELF 12
LISTEN TO YOUR OWN TASTES 13
KNOW THYSELF 13
ACCEPT THE WORLD AS IT IS......................................14
ORIGINAL & UNORTHODOX 14
A SENSE OF PURPOSE & GRATITUDE 15
PRIVATE..16
AUTONOMOUS 16
PEAK EXPERIENCES...17

CHAPTER 3: CHARISMA & LEADERSHIP 18

NO COMMONLY AGREED DEFINITION 19
VISION 20
OBJECTIVE(S) 22
INTEGRITY 23
ACTION-ORIENTATION...25
INTELLIGENCE 26
INDIVIDUALIZED CONSIDERATION 28
MANAGEMENT-BY-EXCEPTION 30

CHAPTER 4: CHARISMA & THE TAO 32

THE STEADY FORCE OF ATTITUDE..................................33
SUBTLE INFLUENCE 34
MAINTAINING SIMPLICITY 34
GRAVITAS..36
COORDINATING COLLECTIVE EFFORT 37
GUIDE RATHER THAN RULE...38
CULTIVATING ONE-NESS...38
UNITY OF EFFORT 39

i

Contents

REPLACE RIGID RULES WITH SPONTANEITY 39
LIKE COOKING A SMALL FISH 40
UNITING THE GROUP INTO A TEAM 41
AVOID MACHIAVELLIAN STRATEGIES 41
HUMILITY 41
COMPASSION 42
AVOID SELF-AGGRANDISEMENT 42
AVOID CUNNING AND MANIPULATION 43
AVOID AGGRESSION 44
USE FORCE ONLY WHEN ABSOLUTELY NECESSARY 44
CULTIVATING RESTRAINT AND HUMILITY 45
KNOWING HOW MUCH IS ENOUGH 45
AVOIDING ESCALATION 46
ACCEPTING BLAME 46
PROMOTING INDEPENDENCE 47

CHAPTER 5: THE LEADERSHIP LITERATURE 48

UNTIL KINGS WERE PHILOSOPHERS 48
DISTINGUISHING LEADERS AND MANAGERS 49
SOCIAL CONSTRUCT OF LEADERSHIP 50
LEADERSHIP QUALITIES OF GREAT GROUPS 51
COMPETENCIES OF EFFECTIVE LEADERS 52
EFFECTIVE MANAGEMENT OF TECHNICAL PEOPLE 54
UNDERLYING QUALITIES OF EFFECTIVE LEADERS 56
EMPATHY 57
PERSONAL RESPONSIBILITY 57
OPEN TO THE TRUTH 58
TRANSFORMATIONAL VS. TRANSACTIONAL 58
PARTICIPATIVE VS. DIRECTIVE 60
REVIEW OF LEADERSHIP FINDINGS 60
LEADERSHIP OF VIRTUAL TEAMS 63
LEADERSHIP OF KNOWLEDGE WORKERS 63
CHALLENGES OF GLOBAL SOFTWARE DEVELOPMENT 66
EFFECTIVE VIRTUAL TEAM LEADERSHIP 67
SLOAN DISTRIBUTED LEADERSHIP MODEL 68

REFERENCES 74

APPENDIX: RHETORICAL DEVICES 78

Introduction

Charisma is an over-used word in the 21st Century. It has come to have several meanings; a compelling attractiveness or charm that inspires devotion, or a divinely conferred power or talent [2]. This book concerns itself with how you can cultivate the character traits that lead to the first meaning.

Charisma can best be understood as an aspect of leadership, the ability to inspire people and make them want to help you realise your vision of the future. While every leader is unique, there are certain underlying qualities that all leaders have. This book presents those qualities. Learn these and in time you can develop your own personal charisma. It is an evolutionary process, not a radical overnight one.

Leadership is an intermediate step in the process. It begins with the very personal quest for self-actualization. Readers may be familiar with this concept from the work of the humanistic psychologist Abraham Maslow [3]. Self-actualization is the natural process of a person reaching their fullest human potential. Maslow recognized it as the highest need that humans have. A person only becomes aware of it when they have satisfied their intermediate and lower needs.

If you sincerely want to develop a magnetic personality, this book can help you towards that goal.

1

Chapter 1: The nature of charisma

Charisma can be thought of as a subtle light that shines from within a person who is living their life to its fullest potential. People respond to this light and want it for themselves so they are drawn to that person. They perceive instinctively that here is someone who has reached an advanced state of self-realization and it is natural that they, the observer, should want that for themselves. After all, it is a human need to become the fullest expression of your human potential.

The qualities of a charismatic person can be summed up quite simply; they are positive (passionately, obsessively so), they see the potential in people and want to help them to achieve it, they envisage a bright future, and they are generous with their time and energies. While you might begin now to emulate these qualities to good effect, you should understand that they are a by-product of a larger process of personal development called *self-actualization*, a broad term covering many aspects of personality (this will be explored in detail in a later chapter).

Being charismatic relies on a person having the emotional intelligence to know how to communicate with people at an emotional level, making a deep, instinctive connection that is not possible at a purely rational level. Emotional intelligence can be a difficult skill to master for people who operate principally on the intellectual level. It involves understanding one's own emotions, how to harness them to solve problems, and how to manage and regulate one's emotions and those of others. In our evolutionary past, going back hundreds of thousands, even millions of years, our primate ancestors operated largely on the emotional level. Emotions are generated by parts of the brain that existed long before those areas that evolved more recently which allow us to think objectively.

The foundation of emotional intelligence is the successful integration of your emotions with your rational mind, making you an integrated whole person. In a sense, it is the integration of the ancient human with the modern human. In broad terms, this involves (a) recognising the emotion, (b) accepting that the emotion exists and is valid, (c) understanding what the emotion is telling us and why, then (d) regulating or managing the emotion so that it comes under the control of the rational mind.

Empathy is the aspect of emotional intelligence that tells us what other people are feeling and perhaps thinking. Empathy is how groups of ancient humans were able to cooperate and adapt in the evolutionary environment. Their survival often depended on it. Charisma needs a strong empathic link to work.

Combine emotional intelligence with a strong sense of purpose and the ability to communicate and you have the makings of a powerfully charismatic person. I'm talking purpose so strong that it burns like a flame and animates your every action. This is purpose invested with powerful emotion that is being constructively channelled. People today instinctively recognize and respond to it just as much they would have in our evolutionary past.

Strong purpose confers on you an air of certainty, and of course the derived confidence that goes with it. Most people are not so confident as this but would like to be so when they encounter someone who does seem to have confidence, they feel like becoming an ally so they can indirectly benefit from the charismatic person's confidence.

Charisma also seems to be an aspect of being self-less. The person engaged in a crusade for a good cause is endowed with a certain aura that others perceive as charisma. The philosopher Daniel Dennett rightly says that *the secret of happiness is to find something more important than yourself and devote your life to it*. Dennett is talking about being happy. It is not too much of a stretch to understand happiness as a strong sense of satisfaction and fulfilment from working tirelessly for the greater good. This is a characteristic of the self-actualized person.

A strong sense of purpose comes from transcending your egoic self and putting yourself at the service of something greater. The selfish ego will not like being diminished and will struggle to reassert itself, and therein lies the battle. The ego can be understood as a survival mechanism that evolved in humans to formulate survival strategies. As useful as the ego once was, today it is an impediment to a person's progress towards self-actualization. The ego is fundamentally selfish because its primary purpose is to ensure its own survival.

Ultimately though, charismatic people have found a way to transcend their egos to some extent and put themselves to work in the service of some greater good.

Charisma is about communicating on an emotional level in ways that connect with the emotions of an audience. The ancient Greeks understood this; the art of Rhetoric became an essential skill to be learned by any educated person. Listen to a recording of any great orator and you will hear their consummate command of rhetoric. Repetition is a favourite technique.

For example, Winston Churchill's *we shall fight on the beaches, we shall fight on the landing grounds, we shall fight in the fields and in the streets, we shall fight in the hills* ... the phrase *we shall fight* is repeated many times to emphasise the determination of the British to warn the invading Germans this would be no easy task.

John F. Kennedy's *Ich bin ein Berliner* speech likewise uses repetition to create an emotional bond between the besieged West Berliners and the American people. Martin Luther King's *I have a dream* speech also uses repetition to very good effect. Many would recognize that all of these speakers were charismatic, each in their way. They each had a powerful message to communicate and they knew how to connect with the emotions of the audience.

This requires rhetorical skills that can be learned (see Appendix for list of rhetorical devices). At the verbal level, charismatic people have a rhythmic, almost hypnotic way of speaking that expresses deep conviction. At the non-verbal level, it means possessing a calm dignity, poise. Nothing perturbs you. This is a powerful combination; an emotionally charged message, calmly delivered.

Charismatic people have *gravitas* (weight, seriousness, dignity, or importance). It makes them seem reserved and virtuous. People are attracted to mystery, particularly when it is coming from a background of simple virtue. Think of how Churchill, Kennedy and King all had a simple, virtuous aim. Their point was clear, anyone could grasp it, so compelling that it would be hard to disagree.

When you show that there is more to you than meets the eye, but you have no desire to display it, people are intrigued. They are drawn to you because they want to know the 'secret' that lets you be that way. It is good practice to not reveal too much of yourself to the world because familiarity breeds contempt in all but your nearest and dearest.

When someone tries to get your attention, pause a moment before looking at them. You turn when you have finished your current train of thought. This calls for careful judgment, wait too long and you appear rude, turn too quickly and you appear nervous.

A steady but non-threatening gaze also contributes to the appearance of charisma. When meeting a person's gaze, you are not the one who looks away first. If it become a staring match, you might decide to continue, or to break the gaze by looking past the other person at something behind them as though this is what you were actually looking. The important point is to not look *down* or *to either side*, as this implies submission to a dominant other.

There are many books and courses available on the market today that promise to teach you how to be charismatic, the easy way. Some of these have value, while others are merely a set of glib techniques that teach you how to fool people into thinking you are charismatic (the *fake it till you make it* approach). In other words, they teach how to outwardly project yourself in certain ways, but without telling you how to transform your inner self so that you naturally project those qualities.

The process takes months and years, the rest of your life perhaps, but that is fine, it is the journey that matters, not some perfect destination. Perfection can never be fully attained, only approached ever more closely. Do not be discouraged though, early encouraging results can be expected.

If months and years seems too long to wait, remember that in five years or ten years you will still be five years or ten years older regardless of how you spend that time, always assuming you live that long.

The best use of your time now is to invest it in something that will bring you long-term benefit, not short-term gratification. Can you honestly think of anything better than becoming a self-actualized, high-achieving, happier and more fulfilled version of the person you are now, someone living at their fullest potential?

Chapter 2: Charisma & self-actualization

This book argues the position that while charisma is perceived as the result of certain outward behaviors, true charisma comes from within the heart and soul of a person who is reaching their fullest potential as a human being. This heightened level of awareness has been called enlightenment, awakening, Satori and many other labels. But these have connotations of mysticism that people in the rational 21st century are uncomfortable with. So let us call it *self-actualization*, the name given to it by humanistic psychologist Abraham Maslow.

The achievement of self-actualisation is recognised by Maslow as a human need; the ultimate destination of the evolved human. This need asserts itself once we have satisfied the lower-order needs for food, shelter, sex, then middle-order needs for safety and security, then love and belonging, and then the higher-order need for self-esteem. Self-actualisation comes next.

The annals of various religions tell us that a person can achieve enlightenment with only some or none of the higher and middle order needs being met, and with only the barest of lower-order needs like food and shelter being satisfied. This is more difficult, requiring you to become an ascetic recluse and engage in mortification of the flesh in order to free yourself of these normal human needs. I am definitely not recommending mortification of the flesh. Our body is not an impediment to self-actualisation.

Characteristics of self-actualized people

Self-Actualized (SA) people, whoever they are and whatever the circumstances of their lives, tend to approach life in recognisable ways that can be described and perhaps emulated. This chapter does not prescribe specific behavior; rather it paints a portrait of the generic self-actualized person that the reader can use to model their own behavior in whatever ways make the most sense to them.

Your challenge is to make the effort to understand each characteristic at a deep level, and find a way of applying it in your own life. Thus it becomes your own, unique way, 100% yours, completely authentic.

This process is likely to takes years, so it is important to adjust your expectations. On the plus side, there can be no greater journey that a person can take than the one that leads to the fullest expression of their human potential.

Experience life wholeheartedly, now

Self-Actualized (SA) people throw themselves unreservedly into the experiences that come their way. They do not hold back. They concentrate on the experience to the exclusion of all else. They do not think, *oh this could be better*, or *I wish I was somewhere else*. They see each moment as perfect in its own way. Recognizing this allows you to then experience the moment wholeheartedly.

See it from an investment point of view. We all know that we receive to the extent that we contribute. By investing fully in the moment, you receive from the moment in equal measure, thus heightening the experience.

There is strong correspondence here with the Buddhist practice of Mindfulness in which you are fully present in the Now moment. Your heightened awareness allows you to fully experience each moment on the understanding that *every moment is the best moment.*

Mindfulness is cultivated by *observing* one's own mind. It leads you to dwell in the present, which is the only time and place where life can *actually* be experienced. The past can only be remembered. The future can only be anticipated. Neither is real in the way that the present is real.

An important element of this present moment awareness is to have a judgment-free mind-set. Judgment creates categories, imposes values. We can get so lost in those thought processes that we are no longer experiencing the reality of the moment, instead a rather tangled mental construct.

Being fully aware, SA people understand that life is a series of moment-by-moment choices between *safety* (out of fear and need for defence) and *risk* (for the sake of progress and growth). You consciously make the growth choice many times a day.

Your primary reality is a rich inner life

Self-Actualized people transcend socially-defined modes of thinking, feeling and acting. They let their inner experience tell them what they truly feel. They do not follow the opinion of the crowd for its own sake, not having much faith in the collective wisdom of the individually ignorant. As harsh as that might sound, the mentality of the crowd usually resides at the lowest common denominator.

SA people live rich inner lives which they recognise as their primary reality. The outer world is their secondary reality. Hence they tend to socialise with those who do not demand sacrifice to group-norms as the price of friendship.

The need for social acceptance and a sense of belonging can lead people to think and act in conventional, group-defined ways. To gain the security of belonging to a group, you usually have to sacrifice your independence of thought, your autonomy, to the group norms.

The SA person transcends the herd mentality and the need for social acceptance, recognizing that such acceptance is a method of control. Society reinforces behavior through approval, and limits other behavior though disapproval. Approval and disapproval are two sides of the same coin. The SA person acknowledges the need for a well-ordered society, but also knows that what was correct in the past may not be correct today. The world has changed since then, and new ways are needed in order to evolve society. The SA person, with their conviction and vision of the future is therefore perceived to have charisma.

Honesty with oneself

It takes courage, but Self-Actualized people look honestly at themselves and take responsibility for who and what they are, and what happens in their life because they have come to be able to see the cause-and-effect links between what they did in the past and what is happening now. Likewise they consciously create a desirable future by creating the causal event now that will result in that future.

Thus they avoid feeling like a victim and remain empowered.

Delusion is the enemy of self-actualisation. Being attached to an incorrect belief leads to suffering, yet *so* many people operate this way. Looking around in the world, it is rare to find people who do not use delusion as a coping mechanism, but SA people recognise that delusion is ultimately self-defeating. Ask yourself, am I ready to hear criticism, even though it will be painful?

SA people have a superior ability to reason, to perceive the truth. They are realistically oriented with an efficient perception of reality extending into all areas of life. They are not frightened by the unknown.

SA people see the truth of the world, recognising the flawed and temporary nature of objects and ideas. They clearly see the cause and effect relationships that connect the events of the world.

Listen to your own tastes

Self-Actualized people are prepared to be unpopular if necessary. As mentioned previously, the need for social acceptance can lead one to compromise one's principles for the sake of getting along.

SA people understand that while compromise on minor issues is often necessary and unavoidable, there is a line that must not be crossed.

Know thyself

Self-Actualized people ask themselves *who am I, what am I, what is good and what is bad for me, where am I going, what is my mission in life?*

Opening up yourself in this way means recognising where your defences and blockages are -- and then finding the courage to give them up.

SA people consciously live their lives in the ways listed above and so they allow their leadership potential to emerge and become established.

The opposite of this is the uncritical mind-set of the person who cruises along through life, making choices based on comfort and security and the conventional wisdom of the society in which they live. They do not know themselves; they are too focussed on what the outside world thinks.

Accept the world as it is

Self-Actualized people see human nature as it really is, and comes to constructive terms with it. They know that it cannot be changed through wishful thinking.

They have rid themselves of the torments of the past. Whether they have hurt others or been hurt, they make amends and resolve firmly to never repeat that behavior. They know that unresolved guilt and shame is a cancer that eats away at their character. Living in the Now helps them to leave the past behind and not re-live it every day.

They enjoy themselves without regret or apology, and have no unnecessary inhibitions.

SA people have realistic or low expectations, so they are rarely disappointed.

Original & unorthodox

Self-Actualized people are unhampered by convention. Their ethics are autonomous, they see themselves as individuals, and are motivated towards continual improvement.

SA people respond to situations appropriately because they perceive the situation clearly and act accordingly, not by replaying a standard response from their behavioral repertoire.

A sense of purpose & gratitude

Charisma has been clearly linked to a strong sense of purpose. Self-Actualized people have a mission in life that requires much energy. Their mission is their reason to be alive. SA people are usually serene and worry-free as they pursue their mission with unshakeable determination.

The SA person's sense of purpose informs almost every aspect of their life. It is their reason to get out of bed in the morning and keeps them hard at work all day, though they probably would not call it work since it is what they would be doing anyway, regardless of whether they need the money.

SA people often feel a deep sense of gratitude for being alive in the world with the skills they possess and the opportunity to use those skills to best effect. Gratitude is perceived as a force of Nature that has a powerfully transformative effect on those who practice it.

Gratitude acknowledges the many good things already in your life and creates the conditions for more to come in. They come because they are appreciated and there is space for them. On the other hand, the person who complains about what they have or do not have is closing the door to further gifts by saying, *I don't like what I have, bring me something better*, sounding like a petulant restaurant patron.

This is the *carpe diem* (seize the day) principle; live each day as if it were your last while gratefully working towards a long and happy future.

Private

Self-Actualized people is alone but not lonely. Solitude is often their preference because in the silence they can hear the wee small voice of their conscience telling them many interesting things.

They are serene, retaining their dignity amid confusion and personal misfortunes. The SA person is deeply introspective, and for this they require privacy, a calm place away from the crowd with its trivial pre-occupations and relentless gossip.

The space that the SA person creates with their privacy is the space in which they can be creative, able to listen to their muse. If they are prevented from expressing their creative output they become very frustrated.

Autonomous

SA people are self-contained, resilient and stable in the face of hard knocks. They are independent from the love and respect of others in the sense that they can resist attempts to use these to manipulate them.

Autonomy does not mean being a law unto oneself. Rather it means being the embodiment of natural law, and as such do not need to look outside of themselves at some external authority to tell them how to act.

Peak experiences

Peak experiences can be compared to becoming enlightened, experiencing Satori. In Maslow's words peak experiences are *'feelings of limitless horizons opening up to the vision, the feeling of being simultaneously more powerful and also more helpless than one ever was before, the feeling of ecstasy and wonder and awe, the loss of placement in time and space with, finally, the conviction that something extremely important and valuable had happened, so that the subject was to some extent transformed and strengthened even in his daily life by such experiences. When peak experiences are especially powerful, the sense of self dissolves into an awareness of a greater unity.'* [2]

Peak experiences are the transcending of ordinary consciousness in which you see yourself as separate from the world, to a state of mind in which you see yourself and everything in the universe as fully inter-connected. It is a feeling of being one with all things.

While you cannot order peak experiences on demand, you can create the right conditions in yourself for them to occur. This characteristics described in this chapter tells you what these conditions are. It does not prescribe a particular way of going about this. To do so would be to limit your freedom to act and inhibit your autonomy. If you are reading this book, you are more than capable of finding your own way of doing these things. In the end, your own unique way is really the only way you should do it.

Chapter 3: Charisma & leadership

Leadership is perhaps the most obvious way that charisma is expressed. Even when someone does not set out to show leadership, their charisma causes them to be perceived as a leader.

People *want* to be shown the way. A small proportion of people, perhaps one in twenty, or 5% insist on being their own person and resist efforts to conform to group-think. The other 95% are actively looking for a leader to tell them how to think and how to act. This is not intended as a judgmental statement; it is simply an observation of human nature. We are a social creature, highly suggestible by the group.

As an undergraduate studying psychology at the University Queensland in the 1980's, a lecturer related a fascinating incident. During the Second World War, the Japanese Army had a problem. They had a large number of prisoners of war who they were obliged to house and guard, and this was a serious drain on their resources. The solution was to isolate in maximum security the 5% of the PoW population who were the natural leaders. The remaining 95% were so docile without their leaders that they needed only minimum security arrangements. The Germans also employed this strategy, establishing Colditz Castle as their supermax prison for the 'incorrigible' 5%. It appears this one in twenty proportion is quite consistent across cultures.

No commonly agreed definition

The phenomenon of leadership has been studied for thousands of years; hardly surprising given its importance and influence in human affairs. Yet despite this sustained interest, no common definition of leadership has yet been agreed. There are many definitions, each one serving a researcher's purposes.

The divergence of opinion can be explained by leadership being *situationally expressed*. It is the circumstances that determine how a leader is perceived. We have seen how a previously unrecognized leader steps up during a time of need. Winston Churchill is a prime example of this. His leadership style was considered to radical before and after World War II, but *during* the war, he was the right man for the job.

Leadership is contingent on a set of personality factors. If these are present in a person, he or she is likely to be perceived as a leader in a wide variety of situations.

After a broad survey of the literature this chapter presents a summary of the basic leadership personality traits that appear again and again in the literature.

These are the *common denominators* of leadership that appear to go across culture and time. It is particularly valuable to recognize these arguably universal factors. Regardless of time and place, these are the qualities that will always be recognised in leaders.

Vision

A charismatic leader has the vision, the insight to see a great future, but it does not end there. They also have the skill to communicate that personal vision to the world so that it becomes a shared vision. People hear this message and think, *yes of course, why didn't I think of that? I want to be part of making this happen.*

Charisma is useful for persuading people to get on board with your idea. Here are some specific ideas that can help translate the vision into a workable set of goals that you and a team might then work towards.

There are three stages to this process:

1. *A vision of the future goal(s) is created.* This vision must be believed to be achievable. The goal will still be abstract at this point.

2. *The vision of the goal(s) is communicated in a way that creates positive expectations in people.*

3. *Commitment to the shared vision is gained.* The way in which the shared vision of the abstract goal(s) is communicated should generate strong commitment to the achievement of the goal(s).

The shared vision is a clear and unambiguous expression of an envisioned future. It is the basis for a common understanding among stakeholders of the aspirations and governing ideals of the team in relation to the desired outcomes. Conditional on being effectively communicated by the leader to the team, the shared vision grounds the team's governing ideas and principles and allows for appropriate objectives to be derived.

Highly effective groups are often convinced they are engaged in important work, sometimes nothing short of being on a 'mission from God'. The work becomes an abiding obsession, a quest that goes well beyond mere employment. This intensely shared vision and sense of purpose endows cohesion and persistence.

The critically important factor here is to give people a strong sense of purpose. They are engaged in work that is bigger and more important than they are.

In summary when putting forth a shared vision, the following factors should be considered:

1.   the project's objectives

2.   the conditions and outcomes the project will create

3.   interfaces the project needs to maintain

4.   the visions created by interfacing groups

5.   the constraints imposed by outside authorities (e.g., environmental regulations)

6.   project operation while working to achieve its objectives (both principles and behaviors)

Objective(s)

Once goals have been created from the compelling vision, it is time to make the goal more concrete by creating a set of objectives that are based on the vision and its derived goals.

Here are some specific ideas that can help translate the goals into a workable set of objectives that can help you and a team:

1. *Practical objective(s) for goal(s) achievement are developed.* From the shared vision and subsequent goals a set of practically-worded objectives are developed that give the team a concrete set of outcomes to achieve.

2. *Positive expectation for achieving objective(s) is encouraged.* having developed concretely-worded objectives, the leader generates in the team an optimistic mind-set and outlook to wards the achievement of the objectives

When the leader has developed a compelling vision of what is to be accomplished, and managed to communicate it in a way that generates enthusiasm and commitment by the team, the leader, in consultation with team members if practical, develops a set of practically-worded objective(s) that explicitly describes what is to be achieved.

Integrity

Integrity is to act with consistency and competence over time in pursuit of the guiding vision and its derived goals and objectives.

People know they can rely on you to always behave in predictable if not ethical ways. Your behavior is a non-verbal affirmation that you value honesty and truth.

Here are some guidelines:

1. *Integrity is consistently practiced.* The leader consistently displays integrity, characterised by openness to truth, trustworthiness, and adherence to principle.

2. *Competence is consistently exhibited.* The leader manifests competence, characterised by technical and interpersonal skills, and advanced conceptual and reasoning skills. Competence in this context can be seen as an aspect of integrity in that it would be dishonest of an incompetent leader to act in a capacity that requires competence.

Integrity-centred leadership creates a climate in which team members can rely on a leader to act according to guiding principle rather than exigent circumstances. Involves doing the 'right thing' all of the time, even when it is easier not to under the circumstances.

Such a leader leads by example, leads by having an open, enlightened mind, leads by remaining true to him/herself.

Such a person is a natural leader, one who is respected and whose example is followed. The antithesis is the tyrant who is closed-minded and who uses force to make people cooperate.

Such a leader acts from a sense of oneness with those being led. This sense of oneness is cultivated in a general sense by learning to recognise the interdependence and connectedness of the group members.

Such a leader avoids using unnecessary force to achieve ends, understanding that to do so create a new set of problems.

Self-worth is encouraged when the leader minimises the perceived distance between their sense of their own position and the position of those they lead. By identifying with the group members the leader can better understand the psychological needs of the members, and so their decisions are more aligned with those needs.

By extension, an effective leader might go so far as to practice humility as a way of engendering the trust and respect of the group members. The interests of the members are naturally promoted because they are the interests of the leader as well. Therefore, effective leaders win the confidence of group members because the members sense the leader's identification with them.

Integrity therefore calls for a high degree of moral courage, since from social psychology we know that people generally act according to who they are with rather than on principle, particularly if doing so will make them unpopular.

Action-orientation

A leader is inclined towards taking action. They know that a person who *can* act but does not is no better than someone who is cannot act in the first place (through lack of ability). Being action-oriented also means being resilient. Trying and not succeeding is no reason to give up. The action-oriented leader keeps trying, learning from their mistakes until success is achieved.

1. *Objective-achieving behavior is decisively pursued.* The leader consistently displays the ability to think and act decisively in pursuit of objective(s).

2. *Objective-frustrating events are met with resilience.* When progress is frustrated the leader consistently displays a willingness to try again until success is achieved.

3. *Viability of continuing pursuit of current objective(s) is evaluated.* The previous outcome notwithstanding, when it becomes clear that a course of action is no longer viable and the pursuit of which is unwise, the leader rationally evaluates whether continued pursuit is advisable.

Action-oriented leaders are able to overcome the inertia and disincentives inherent in situations that lesser people might succumb to. Action-orientation is particularly relevant in goal-frustrating situations when others might give up.

Action-oriented implies taking action when necessary, and refraining from action when none is required – the 'leave well-enough alone' principle. In this way, the leader gains the confidence and trust of the group by being calm and in control.

Leaders are more likely to develop resilience when their guiding vision is strong enough to remain in force even when an alternative situation has been imposed, and which threatens the realization of the goal. The leader has the integrity and the strength of character to remain true to the original goal in the face of adversity.

Intelligence

An effective leader makes good use of their full repertoire of cognitive resources in pursuit of their objectives.

Specifically:

1. *Original thinking in team-members is facilitated.* The leader encourages a high-level of original thinking in the team, enabling new solutions to problems to be developed, unbounded by orthodoxy. This can be achieved by explicitly encouraging thinking beyond the conventional, setting the expectation that this will be so. The leader can reward original thinking. In short, it becomes a group-norm.

2. *Situations are realistically understood.* The leader displays a realistic understanding of situations, which enables appropriate action to be taken.

Appropriate in this sense means leading to the achievement of objectives.

3. *Cause(s) of objective-achieving outcomes are generated.* The leader takes action to generate the circumstances or causes that lead to the achievement of objectives. In other words, engineering the right conditions for objectives to be achieved.

Abstract conceptualization is an aspect of intelligence that allows a leader to mentally manipulate abstractions in problem-solving, efficiency-enhancing ways. This is related to the ability to create a unifying vision for the project, which can be seen as a higher level abstract conceptualization skill. The skill being discussed in this process relates more to how to make it happen.

Without necessarily dispensing with the benefits of accumulated experience and lessons learned, creative, unorthodox thinking can lead to solutions that are beyond the reach of conventional thinking. Persistent problems usually require new ways of thinking. Original thinkers are not so influenced by the opinions of those that say 'it cannot be done', they are more likely to think 'we haven't thought of a way yet'. It is to be free from the restraints of tradition - the 'wisdom of the ages' that can be a straightjacket for the mind.

A leader who follows this approach allows the team to function naturally, in proper response to the conditions in which it finds itself. In contrast, a tradition-bound leader will base his decisions on precedent; 'what did my predecessors do in this situation'. These prefabricated responses lack insight and run a high risk of not being appropriate for the situation at hand.

Good judgment is a fundamental ability that informs almost all of a leader's activities. It is the foundation of appropriate action. Good judgment is conditional upon a rational, objective mind-set in which people, objects and events are viewed realistically for what they are in any particular set of circumstances, rather than relying on stereotypes and prescribed understandings to guide their actions.

Accepting responsibility requires the courage to accept the truth or reality of a situation, even when it is unpleasant. Effective leaders accept that the circumstances in which they find themselves are largely the result of their own previous actions. They do not blame others. They are able to see the linkages between cause and effect, how their behavior affects corporate vision and how their leadership can affect the profitability of the organisation. Effective leaders are proactive, rather than reactive, taking the initiative to improve matters.

Individualized consideration

Effective leaders know that people respond most positively when they known as a whole person, not merely as a unit of production. The leader makes the effort to get to know people at a personal level, letting them see that they are valued and appreciated for who they are.

1. *Individual team-members are valued.* The leader manifests an understanding of team-members from within a mind-set of respect. This leads to a valuing of the member as an individual. On perceiving this mind-set in the leader, the person's commitment is reinforced.

2. *Individual team-members are unified into team.* The leader engenders a sense of unity in the team. A 'group-mind' that thinks as one mind and makes them a single entity. The team-members' performance is enhanced by this sense of oneness with the team.

3. *Empathy towards individual team-members is practiced.* The leader empathises with team members to understand their individual experiences and general situation. This ability to place oneself in the shoes of another reinforces the perception in the team-member that they are understood and valued.

4. *Objective-achieving team behavior is rewarded.* The leader encourages goal-achieving behavior in the team by rewarding such behavior. By implication negative reinforcement is avoided unless absolutely necessary. The absence of positive reinforcement functions in place of negative, and avoids resentment build-up in team-members.

Team members recognize that the leaders to some extent knows them as an individual. The antithesis of this is the leader that regards them as expendable units of production.

The leader recognizes the individual talents of team members, and unites them into a single enterprise.

Empathy is distinct from sympathy. Sympathy involves becoming emotionally attached to people and outcomes, whereas empathy is dispassionate, non-judgmental. An analogy from the medical domain is that of a doctor using empathy to accurately understand a patient's condition/situation. The doctor cannot sympathise with the patient if they are not to be overwhelmed by the deluge of suffering they encounter in the course of a day.

In behavioral psychology terms, rewarding desirable performance implies positive reinforcement for desirable behavior. A common mistake is to take desirable performance for granted, effectively ignoring it, while taking action to punish when undesirable performance occurs. While necessary to do the latter on occasion, it must be remembered that the leader's attention is a reward in itself and adopting a reward for desirable performance approach shows significant benefits.

Management-by-exception

An effective leader gives the team the resources and the authority they need to get the job done, and then they step back and let them get on with it, intervening only when the team gets off-track. It is the opposite of micro-management. This model is used to good effect in organisations like Google, and Richard Branson's various Virgin enterprises. Management by exception is contingent on the leader having the discretion to hire the right people for the job, rather than people allocated by centralised authority, some of whom may be under-performers who are not wanted elsewhere.

1. *Independent team behavior that is objective-achieving is encouraged.* When the team is doing their job the leader leaves them alone. In effect, the leader does not give the impression of being a 'micro-manager'. If the team is inexperienced, coaching of specific skills towards objective(s) achievement is warranted. The leader should evaluate the potential negative impact of such coaching before performing.

2. *Non-objective-achieving team behavior is corrected.* The leader takes action to correct the behavior of team members when they engage in non-objective-achieving behavior. When they have gotten 'off the track' or gone 'off on a tangent'. This corrective action must be done with an attitude of respect, and should not resemble negative reinforcement except in extreme or repeated instances.

Management by exception is an empowering approach when a person is expected to act independently, with a degree of autonomy. The person might be a sub-contractor who maintains a professional approach to his/her work and can be relied upon to perform professionally and to a high standard.

Chapter 4: Charisma & the Tao

The essence of leadership is to see a compelling future. Charisma then helps you to communicate your vision of that future in a way that creates excitement.

Self-actualization can help you become charismatic, while the Taoist perspective helps with understanding leadership. It does this by cultivating a strong awareness of the patterns of Nature and how these influence human societies. With this awareness you can extrapolate these patterns into the future and see what is both possible and likely. But the future is not set in stone. Its direction is influenced by the visionaries and their ability to make their vision a reality.

Consider for example the visions of the future created by the early science fiction writers Jules Verne and H.G. Wells. Generations of engineers have been inspired by the works of Verne and Wells, producing all manner of technologies from submarines called *Nautilus* that could travel 20,000 leagues under the sea without surfacing, journeys to the moon and back, and the exploration of Mars. Later sci-fi writers like Philip K. Dick and William Gibson have also had a profound effect on the direction of technology development.

Form and content aside, all of these writers imagined a compelling future and communicated it to the world with impact.

Regardless of whether you are a manager of other people, or someone who has less formal relationships with those around you, the principles discussed in this chapter describe the Taoist way of influencing people. Lao Tzu wrote the Tao Te Ching specifically for those who might help create a better world, those whose position in society was to lead. By default, the Tao Te Ching is a Leadership manual, albeit one that ranges far and wide into all aspects of life itself.

The steady force of attitude

Leading by example is the most desirable form of leadership. The enlightened leader understands that it is the steady force of their attitudes, as perceived by those around them, that exerts the greatest influence, more so than their actions or their words. Through example, people come to know what a leader respects and values. These values become the motivating force behind people's actions. The enlightened leader therefore models high regard for honesty, flexibility and spontaneity.

The enlightened leader avoids championing high-achievers. They know that by creating one winner, they simultaneously create multiple losers who then feel under-valued. High achievers should be quietly congratulated and rewarded. Singling high-achievers out for public praise creates what Stephen Covey calls a scarcity mentality. The praise of the leader is a scarce commodity that is reserved for the favoured few.

The enlightened leader brings peace and stability to the group through the steady force of their positive attitudes. They do not micro-manage, allowing people to get on with their activities without interference.

Subtle influence

According to Lao Tzu, the best kind of leader is one whose existence is barely known by those they lead. The next best are loved, the next are respected and the next are ridiculed.

The enlightened leader avoids coercion, instead they use subtle influence (like goal-setting, trust and carefully worded directives) so that the people are barely aware of their influence. The worst thing a leader can do is adopt and overbearing approach in which people perceive that they are being interfered with at some level and their need for autonomy over how they perform their work is disregarded. This is sure to generate negative reaction.

Subtle influence allows a person to develop autonomy from which they derive the satisfaction of one who manages their own affairs.

Maintaining simplicity

Simple, intuitively-derived ways of behaving that are in tune with the Tao are preferable to socially-defined behaviour protocols. It is all too easy with the latter to make mistakes and give unintentional offence. Correct behaviour protocols create in-groups and out-groups, those who know how to behave correctly, and the uncouth oafs who do not. It plays into the egoic tendency to categorise the world as us and them, friend and enemy. Simple, intuitively based leadership is likely to be more inclusive and compassionate, seeking commonality between people rather than points of difference.

Modes of social behaviour that are considered praiseworthy, such as self-seeking philanthropy, should be avoided. Self-seeking behaviour of any kind is primarily done for social recognition that then feeds back to improved self-esteem. It is an indication that Intuition is not being used and the person needs an external source to tell them what is right and good. The enlightened leader, in tune with their Intuition, practices anonymous philanthropy and enhances their self-esteem directly.

The enlightened leader therefore acts with humility and remains in close contact with their instincts. They keep their thoughts and actions simple and spontaneous. With this mind-set, they are more agile and appropriate in their responses to emerging situations. Simplicity endows power through clarity of meaning. People intuitively perceive the enlightened leader's alignment with the Tao.

The enlightened leader therefore throws off the constraints of orthodoxy and tradition, using these only in a secondary sense, if at all. Orthodoxy can be a straight-jacket for the imagination. It constrains creativity and limits spontaneity. A tradition-bound leader will tend to base their decisions on precedent what did my predecessors do in this situation or in

1793, our illustrious leader did this in response to a similar situation?. These prefabricated responses lack insight and run a high risk of not being appropriate for the situation at hand.

Gravitas

Gravitas or force of personality can exercise strong influence on people, so it is wise to know how to cultivate it. Gravitas is manifested in the enlightened leader as they become more closely aligned with the Tao. Such alignment naturally deepens and endows perceived substance to their personality.

It has been observed that the worth of a nation, or organisation or individual can be known by how they treat the weakest member of their group. Observe how a person treats those over whom they have power. Do they treat them with consideration and respect, or are they harsh because they can be? The enlightened leader knows that treating everyone with simple dignity endows their actions with subtle but powerful influence; the underlying quality of gravitas. Author John Steinbeck demonstrated true leadership with his Nobel Prize winning novel *The Grapes of Wrath* (1939). In contrast, French Queen Marie-Antoinette from her privileged position showed contemptuous disregard for the welfare of the people with her let them eat cake comment. Though probably a journalistic cliché it nonetheless sums up the attitude of the French aristocracy that so enraged the people and led to the French Revolution in 1789.

Enlightened leaders do not use their position to grant themselves special rewards not available to everyone, for example executive bonuses that are many times the annual salary of ordinary employees. The simple dignity of the servant leader is most conducive to achieving their objectives.

Coordinating collective effort

Enlightened leadership is seen where the talents and abilities of a diverse set of people can be coordinated into a unified effort. Such leadership is about creating an environment in which people can network and exchange ideas in pursuit of common objectives. The leader is like a lake that collects and contains water. They modestly provide the environment in which people can work together and exchange ideas in pursuit of common objectives. Their influence is so pervasive and subtle that people stop noticing it.

Intuitive leaders therefore have the ability to unite people with diverse backgrounds into a single enterprise, thus creating a direct link between people whose only previous connection was so tenuous as to be almost invisible. The enlightened leader perceives these subtle connections and builds networks out of them. In this way, they behave like the Tao.

Guide rather than rule

It is well-known that people dislike being forced to do anything. They prefer freedom to choose, or at least the appearance of freedom. So even when an enlightened leader has the authority to order people about, they avoid doing so. They know it is better to guide people to a course of action by giving them a reason to want to do it. As Dwight Eisenhower remarked, leadership is the art of getting people to do what you want them to do because they want to do it. The enlightened leader does this by presenting the case in such a way that the course of action is clearly in the person's best interest and/or the greater interests of the group they serve.

Cultivating one-ness

The enlightened leader recognises the inter-connectedness of all things in the universe and cultivates a sense of solidarity and oneness with people.

This oneness is a state of felt awareness and harmony between the one and the many. The enlightened leader works daily to cultivate and maintain this sense of felt connectedness with everything. It gives insight into the rhythms and patterns of the Universe and informs the enlightened leader's every action.

Unity of effort

Unity of effort is achieved when the enlightened leader creates enthusiasm for their vision of the future. They put the right person in the job, provide the resources they need, the authority to make decisions, then stand back and let them do the work without unnecessary restrictions.

Lao Tzu believed that people are basically good at heart, only becoming aggressive and unruly in reaction to unreasonable force or perceived injustice. The enlightened leader therefore fosters a collaborative environment based on fairness and behaves with simplicity and modesty. They avoid creating unnecessary internal competition which works against collaboration by encouraging people to pursue strategies to gain advantage at the expense of others.

Replace rigid rules with spontaneity

Some organisations operate with rigidly defined rules that everyone must conform to if they are not to be punished. This approach offends human nature that is angered by unreasonable force. The consequence is that the people grow resentful and look for ways to subvert the orthodoxy, and they will usually succeed at this. When management perceives the trend, they react by exerting more pressure. The people react even more strongly, and a negative cycle of behaviour is created.

Rigidly defined rules are a form of extremism that produces sharply polarised attitudes. These attitudes are likely to be counter-productive by reducing the desire to collaborate freely. The enlightened leader knows how polarity operates in Nature, and so the avoid such extremes. They achieve their objectives without confrontation, projecting a straight-forward, down-to-earth honesty that inspires trust and confidence in people, and which provides a model for the people to emulate.

Like cooking a small fish

Leading a large organisation is like cooking a small fish. This enigmatic statement conveys the need for an enlightened leader to maintain a light, delicate touch in their leadership in the same way as it is necessary to avoid too much stirring when cooking a small fish, lest the fish fall apart in the pan. When an organisation is experiencing challenges, too much action from the leader will unbalance the situation, making it worse.

The enlightened leader knows that if there is no simple solution to a problem, it is best to simply let it be and allow the forces of Nature to evolve a solution. In this culture of simplicity and non-interference, people engaging in subterfuge become apparent, and their strategies are rendered ineffective.

Uniting the group into a team

The enlightened leader makes it their business to help everyone in the organisation towards fulfilment and higher attainment, not just those that seem somehow worthy of preferment. Lesser performers are also regarded as valuable members of the group who can be helped forward with education and other opportunities. This transforms a group into a team who are united behind the leader, and in whom the desire to collaborate is strong.

Avoid Machiavellian strategies

The enlightened leader refrains from clever strategies and political manoeuvrings. They know that this sends a message to do likewise, leading to an escalating cycle of such behaviour in the organisation. The enlightened leader therefore acts with simplicity and directness and so encourages the people to do likewise.

Humility

The enlightened leader understands that to rise above people in a leadership sense, they must remain below them by acting and speaking with sincere humility. This is perceived as complete identification with the people, engendering trust because the people instinctively know that if the leader is below them, the interests of the leader will be the same as theirs. If the leader does not act superior, the people see themselves in the leader and this engenders respect, if not love.

Compassion

The best kind of leader is compassionate, modest and does not thrust themselves into the lime-light. Lao Tzu considered that compassion in a person has a mysterious and deeply transformative effect on the mind of the person and those they come in contact with. Compassion endows the ability to have a lasting effect on the world. The enlightened leader therefore manifests compassion in their dealings with the world.

Avoid self-aggrandisement

Enlightened people avoid being too visible or boastful of their achievements because there is a levelling mechanism in group psychology that naturally seeks to balance aggrandisement. Such behaviour creates excess. It creates instability in the social dynamic. Excess indicates that something has reached its peak and must by necessity go into decline. The enlightened leader discretely removes themselves from the situation before the limelight shines upon them. For example, even the most popular political leader is harshly criticised by sections of the public, regardless of how diligently they work to stay in favour.

Hypocrisy is particularly poisonous. The enlightened leader carefully avoids not only being a hypocrite, but the appearance of being one. They know it is tempting to agree with people in private discussions, expressing a different opinion with each person, as a way of earning their support. But the enlightened leader knows that they must maintain the integrity of their position, and not vary it between people.

This sameness of bearing towards everyone generates trust. Even though this may not please everyone, it does earn the enlightened leader a reputation for integrity and impartiality. Often, the person of integrity pleases no-one, and is criticised for it because they refuse to take sides in a dispute. It is the only viable way to behave however, since any favours earned through double-dealing are short-lived. The friend of today becomes an enemy tomorrow. The person of integrity earns the respect of all, if not their friendship.

Avoid cunning and manipulation

Clever schemes and coercive force will often produce the opposite of what was planned, earning the person a reputation for cunning and duplicity. The enlightened leader knows it is better to act with simple honesty in pursuit of one's goals, thus generating trust.

Simplicity is achieved through spontaneous, intuitive action based on an understanding of human nature and the situation at hand. This is the opposite of the Machiavellian ploy that may succeed in the short-term, but not in the mid to long-term.

Avoid aggression

Aggression in all of its forms is avoided by the enlightened leader, since aggression creates excess, and excess always produces a neutralising reaction. Where affirmative action is called for, the enlightened leader behaves assertively, not crossing the line between aggression and assertion. Assertion is restrained action.

Aggression in individuals and groups consumes much energy and resources, leading to resource depletion and weakening. Restrained action uses that energy constructively in the pursuit of its goals. The enlightened leader knows that success does not have to come at the expense of another. The win-win scenario in which everyone benefits is in keeping with the Tao.

Use force only when absolutely necessary

When circumstances demand it, the use of force can be unavoidable. The enlightened leader expresses regret at having to use force. They make it clear that it gives them no pleasure. As in Nature, the incidence of overwhelming force is rare (for example a tornado or earthquake). Most of the time, change is brought about through harmonious transformation.

Cultivating restraint and humility

Powerful organisations have much in the way of assets and resources, but they also have much to lose. Their wealth and influence are the envy of others who want some of it for themselves. Such organisations can avoid this by cultivating modesty. They make themselves vulnerable to decline through complacency, excess, and sense of entitlement. Hubris leads them to believe they are unassailable. Any advantages the organisation possesses are kept concealed, out of sight from the external world where they will excite no envy or alarm.

Knowing how much is enough

Greed is a serious character flaw. It leads a person to not only desire more possessions, but to seek an identity for themselves in those possessions rather than focus on internal growth. When organisations are run without acquisitiveness as its central concern the internal qualities of the organisation are encouraged to grow in positive, self-improving ways. Its dealings with the world will take on a benevolent aspect which is likely to produce greater prosperity for all and limit the potential for harm.

Avoiding escalation

In any evolving social environment there will be conflict between opposing ideas. The enlightened leader knows that the ideas that eventually prevail are those whose proponents have managed to avoid strong counter-reactions to the idea. They do this by avoiding aggression. Force is met with force, and strategy with strategy. Lao Tzu thought that the side that was wise enough to feel sorrow and regret at the use of force would be the side that triumphs.

Accepting blame

The enlightened leader in organisations takes on the qualities of water. Soft and receptive with no edge and no form, water absorbs and transforms hard structures. By taking responsibility, including accepting the blame for situations, the enlightened leader establishes their position at the centre of the organisation. They extend their influence outwards in a positive way. Blame in this context refers to that which happens inside and outside the organisation. They are able to foresee and avoid similar problems in the future.

Promoting independence

Lao Tzu considered the ideal social grouping (at every level from family to nation) to be one in which every member can reach their potential in whichever direction that takes them. They have access to health care, education and recreation; nothing short of the pursuit of happiness.

Every person values their life, so they will value life-enhancing activities that they instinctively know is the way to find themselves, develop a strong sense of purpose and ultimately reach their full potential. When a person feels strong and independent they are likely to work hard, maintain good relationships and remain loyal to the organisation.

Chapter 5: The leadership literature

This chapter is a summary of the leadership literature. It is an abridged version of the literature review from the author's PhD thesis. It is included in this book so you can see that the material presented is based in part on academic research. Academic language has been moderated for a general readership.

Until kings were philosophers

Until 'kings were philosophers or philosophers were kings' there will be injustice in the world. (Plato)

The classical period of ancient Greece is widely recognized as having produced concepts and modalities that are the bedrock of western civilisation. The philosopher Plato (427-347 BC) in his renowned dialogue *The Republic* outlined certain leadership principles that Western administrative thinking has based itself upon [5] . Plato developed systematic administrative thinking for the efficient running of the city-sate (polis) which over time allowed the evolution of democracy. Plato described in detail the appropriate relationship between the State and individual citizens. This relationship was so close that it was not possible to think of a citizen living outside of his State[5]. The purpose (telos) of this

State is to educate people to become 'good'. The State is like the human body in which parts complement each other and act harmoniously. In terms of organisational theory, Plato would be regarded as a pre-modern functionalist.

In perhaps his best known tract *The Republic* (Polis), Plato states that politicians are the rulers of the new ideal state because they have (or should have) real knowledge (episteme) of what is 'the form of good'.

The art of ruling (leadership) can be based on scientific principles. In other words, it can be learned. The leader (ruler) uses the dialectic method to rationally analyse situations to determine appropriate courses of action with wisdom and understanding.

Distinguishing leaders and managers

The terms leader and manager are sometimes used interchangeably, adding to the ambiguity surrounding the study of leadership. Yet studies of administrative science usually find the terms differentiated. How is this done?

Chaos and order. Abraham Zeleznik [6] in his seminal paper on leadership suggests that the differences between managers and leaders lie at a deep level of the human psyche. Attitudes towards chaos and order are the basis of the difference. A manager aims for stability and control, seeking to resolve problems quickly, sometimes at the cost of understanding the nature of the problem fully. Leaders, by contrast, accept or at least tolerate chaos and lack of structure so that they might perceive and come to understand the underlying causes of situations. In this sense, Zeleznik argues, leaders have more in common with creative thinkers such as artists and scientists than they do with managers.

According to Takala [5] what managers and leaders have in common is the ability to get things done. Takala distinguishes them by seeing managers as a kind of instructor who puts pieces together, and then manages the 'things'. A manager is primarily concerned with making an organisation function by evolving routines that serve the ongoing and sometimes changing purposes of the organisation. Takala [5] observes that management is an activity typical in *larger* corporations. But there is leadership in *every* organisation, and not only in business organisations. A leader is a person who takes care of people and emphasises in his/her activities the social psychology of the organisation. Takala [5] notes that this is a somewhat artificial but commonplace distinction made in the management literature between the two activities. He acknowledges however that a person who runs a business or leads an organisation acts situationally in both roles, sometimes a manager, sometimes a leader.

Social construct of leadership

The socially constructed view holds that leadership is a myth, a socially constructed agency that reinforces existing social beliefs about the need for hierarchy [7]. A consequence of this view is the de-skilling of people, the placing of them into positions of subservience in order that they might follow the leader. Evidence of this is seen in the popular wish for heroes and messianic figures who will save the people and usher in a brighter future [7]. Despite the rather bleak nature of this position, it can nonetheless be observed that members of some organisations do behave like 'alienated robots' in their work relationships.

Leadership qualities of great groups

Bennis and Beiderman [8] discuss at length the leadership qualities required in Great Groups. They observe that the nature of group leaders can vary widely. There are facilitators, doers, contrarians. Leaders are catalytic completers; taking on roles that nobody else plays and that are needed for the group to achieve its goal. They have an intuitive understanding of the 'chemistry' of the group and the dynamics of the work process. Furthermore they encourage dissent in the establishment and maintenance of a shared vision. They can distinguish between healthy, creative dissent and self-serving obstructionism.

Bennis and Beiderman [8] identify four behavioral traits of effective group leaders:

Provide direction and meaning. Group members are kept up-to-date on what is important and why their work makes a difference.

Generate and sustain trust. The group has trust in itself and its leadership. This allows members to accept dissent and tolerate the turbulence of the group process.

Display a bias toward action, risk taking, and curiosity. A sense of urgency and willingness to risk failure to achieve results.

Are purveyors of hope. Find tangible and symbolic ways to demonstrate that the group can overcome difficulties.

Competencies of effective leaders

Bennis [9] in a wide-ranging study determined that effective leaders display four distinct personality traits, and five specific competencies, the sum of which tends to manifest in strong and effective leadership:

Personality Traits	Competencies
Guiding vision	Technical competence
Passion	Interpersonal skills
Integrity	Conceptual skills
Daring	Judgment
	Character

No pairing order is implied by this table, it is a listing only.

Table 1: Traits of Effective Leaders.

Bennis [10] asserts that it is *character* that is the essential element determining a leader's effectiveness, saying *'leaders rarely fail because of technical incompetence'* but more so for lack of character [11].

Strong character can manifest in positive and negative ways, as the lessons of history inform us. Strong character makes for a strong leader, but character can be strong and negative/destructive. Offerman et al [12] relates that a person's character will be determined by the sum total of his or her values. Offerman et al [12] identified the source of an employee's dissatisfaction and disillusionment is often the particular values held by leaders and the actions that these values motivate.

Davis and Landa [13] surveyed workers across Canada, determining that 75% of Canadian employees did not trust their employers. Bennis [10] confirms the importance of trust by emphasising that employee confidence in leadership is critical in the workplace, saying that it is *'the emotional glue that can bond people to an organization.'*

Branham [14] surveyed 3,149 people who voluntarily quit their job to assess their reasons for leaving. The exiting employees cited the following common reasons:

- Disappointment,

- Frustration,

- Anger,

- Disillusionment,

- Resentment, and

- Betrayal

These negative emotions are thought to be responses to an unmet human need for:

- Trust,

- Hope,

- A sense of worth, and

- The need to feel competent

It might therefore follow that an effective leader is someone who is able to meet these fundamental human needs, avoiding the trap that awaits a less effective leader.

Effective management of technical people

The seminal figure of Watts Humphrey looms large in the history of software engineering. His contributions include the original Software Capability Maturity Model CMM-SW), Team Software Process (TSP) and Personal Software Process (PSP); all of which were developed while with the Software Engineering Institute's Process Program.

A lesser known, but nonetheless relevant work by
Humphrey is *Managing Technical People* [24]. While this work is
based on Humphrey's experience as a senior project manager
with the IBM Corporation, rather than on empirical research,
it serves as a validation device for empirical research, given
his undoubted stature in the software engineering domain.
'Validation' is used here in the software engineering sense,
meaning to check the truth and accuracy of something in the
practical world.

To summarise the behaviors and qualities of effective
managers of technical teams, Humphrey [15] observes that:

- **Vision.** The ability to clearly perceive a worthy goal
  in terms of organisational success, and which has the
  quality of making people want to be part of the effort
  to make it real.

- **Goals.** Identified from the vision and the ability to
  drive steadfastly towards their realisation.

- **Conviction.** The ability to overcome obstacles in the
  path towards goal achievement.

- **Attract followers.** The ability to persuade others to
  sign-up or otherwise commit to a project, subject to
  limitations of choice. Humphrey distinguishes
  between the power to control and the power to lead.
  The latter is a mutual relationship, while the former
  implies coercion.

- **Care about followers.** A leader manifests an interest
  in the lives of, and a concern for the well-being of

those they lead (what has been called 'individualised consideration').

- **Transform followers.** To convince followers to dedicate themselves to a project, sometimes requiring great personal effort, the net effect of which is to transform all concerned into high-achievers who derive much satisfaction from the transformative process (elsewhere described as transformational leadership).

- **Transact followers.** Use transactional power (power to reward with increased salary, promotion, job assignments) to effectively motivate followers.

- **Lead from below.** The ability to motivate followers to act as leaders in their own jobs, regardless of how modest or limited in scope this may be. The cumulative effect is nonetheless powerful.

Underlying qualities of effective leaders

The qualities that inspire people to persevere in the face of great difficulty, that engender trust and a sense of worth among team members are not always readily identifiable. These are qualities that are not easily detected, but which are found in the best of leaders.

Champy [16] identify these underlying qualities as:

- Empathy,

- Personal responsibility, and

- Openness to discovering truth

Empathy

Macaluso [17] suggests that empathy is the secret weapon of corporate success, an indispensable quality for any successful leader. Empathy is described as the ability to see the world through another's eyes, to experience it as they would. 'To walk a mile in another's shoes'. Macaluso [17] says 'They use it to form strong relationships, pick up early warning signs, and recognize opportunities to influence.' It is this caring aspect of the leader that makes people want to stay with them, inspiring loyalty.

Personal responsibility

Effective leaders accept that the circumstances in which they find themselves are largely the result of their own previous actions. They recognise the cause and effect relationships that have created the current situation, and understand how to engineer future desirable effects by performing certain actions in the present. They do not blame others [17]. They are able to see how their behavior affects corporate vision and how their leadership can affect the profitability of the organisation. Effective leaders are proactive, rather than reactive, taking the initiative to improve matters [17].

Open to the truth

Effective leaders fearlessly search for truth, knowing that sometimes the truth will not be pleasant to face [17]. They encourage discussion and do not resile from the outcomes of those discussions. The value of truth is recognised as the supreme antidote to delusion, or wishful thinking.

Macaluso [17] concludes with the point that really effective leaders are those that maximise human capital by displaying empathy, personal responsibility and truthfulness in all of their dealings. These traits appear to engender in people a favourable emotional state that is the foundation for effective team operation.

Transformational vs. Transactional

Zhang, Fjermestad and Tremaine [18] identify two parallel dimensions of leadership: *transformational vs. transactional,* and *participative vs. directive.* These have been derived from a body of foundational work in the area of leadership styles in a virtual team context.

On the Transformational / Transactional dimension we see the Transformational element as comprising four behavioral components [19] [20] [21]:

- **Charisma or idealized influence.** The leader engenders in the members a sense of pride, respect, faith and respect, together with a sense of purpose/mission.

- **Individualized consideration.** The leader manifests a deep concern for the well-being of team members, and provides mentoring.

- **Intellectual stimulation.** The leader stimulates members to think in original ways, emphasising the triumph of reason over irrationality, and challenging established ways of thinking.

- **Inspirational motivation.** The leader creates high standards, communicating high expectations.

Continuing with the Transformational / Transactional dimension we see the Transactional element as comprising three behavioral elements [19] [20] [21]:

- **Contingent reward.** The leader rewards performance on the basis of it having fulfilled prescribed obligations.

- **Management-by exception.** The leader ensures the standards are met.

- **Management-by-exception (passive).** The leader adopts a *laissez-faire* attitude until non-compliance of standards has occurred.

Participative vs. directive

On the participative vs. directive dimension, Bass [22] defines participative leadership as the equalization of power and sharing of problem solving with followers by consulting them before making a decision.

Bass [22] defines directive leadership as providing and seeking compliance with directions for accomplishing a problem solving task. Participative leadership and directive leadership are considered parallel to transformational leadership and transactional leadership respectively.

Review of leadership findings

Zhang, Fjermestad and Tremaine [18] discuss at length the findings from various literatures about the distinctions that can be made between Transformational / Transactional and Participative / Directive Leadership styles.

Bass and Avolio [23] discuss that in general, supportive, encouraging communication from the leader to team members were made under participative leadership rather than directive leadership. In dealing with a semi-structured or poorly defined problem, proposed solutions were more forthcoming in a participative leadership situation. On the other hand, solutions to structured or well-defined problems were more forthcoming with directive leadership [23].

In terms of group effectiveness or potency, higher level transformational leadership resulted in greater effectiveness than lower levels of transformational leadership [24]. The group potency difference was larger when groups were engaged in interdependent tasks rather than independent tasks. Interdependence resulted in greater potency. Anonymous groups working under high transformational leadership and identified groups working under low transformational leadership were most effective [24].

Elaboration (or the extent to which work was developed to a higher degree of complexity) was observed to improve significantly; while originality improved marginally when higher levels of transformational leadership were present [25]. Moreover, identified groups or teams with high transformational leadership were more flexible than identified groups in low transformational situations. Flexibility tended to vanish when groups were anonymous [25].

Lim, Raman and Wei [36] indicate that anonymity by itself does not alter the effects of leadership style on (a) participation, (b) cooperation or (c) the originality of the solution. With transactional leadership, anonymity was negatively associated with participation and association due to social loafing (idle chit-chat, gossip etc), but it was positively related to originality of solutions when a group reward as opposed to an individual reward situation exists [26]. It appears that giving member's time to engage in apparently idle communication when group-based solutions are rewarded results in more focussed outcomes. With transformational leadership, anonymity did not significantly change the rate or degree of participation, cooperation, and originality when a group rewards situation exists (as opposed to an individual rewards condition) [26]. Team member satisfaction with the leader did not apparently differ across leadership styles; however transactional leadership did appear to result in greater group efficacy and task satisfaction than does transformational leadership. These advantages associated with transactional leadership (over transformational leadership) diminished when anonymity was introduced.

Team members working under the influence of transformational leaders tended to produce quality over quantity [27]. Output improved, though the quantity of it decreased. Members also tended to be more satisfied and displayed greater group cohesiveness than those led by transactional leaders [27]. Leadership satisfaction (highest in the face-to-face setting) was relatively high in virtual environments that approached full-immersion. Transformational leadership was associated with higher levels of trust in the leader and value congruence [27].

McColl-Kennedy and Anderson [28] report that both participative and directive leaderships were positively related to degree of participation. These in turn produced higher team performance, but with paradoxically lower levels of leadership satisfaction. The positive relationship between participation and team performance as well as the negative relationship between participation and team performance became stronger as the problem turned to be less structured [28].

Leadership of virtual teams

The concept and practice of distributed work is not new, enjoying a long and colourful history as discussed by O'Leary, Orlikowski and Yates [29] in their extended case study of the Hudson Bay Company from 1670 to 1826. Yet it has been the advent and subsequent advances in communications technology that has been a critical enabler of the development of this organisational form and practice [30].

It has been observed [31] that distributed teams, (or virtual teams as they might be called), face particular problems in relation to leadership. Organisational and management research has focussed intensively on the issue of leadership, as seen in a previous section, yet there is relatively little research done thus far on the emerging challenge of leadership in virtual teams [31].

Leadership of knowledge workers

Discussion of leadership in the globalized economy of the 21st century is not complete without examination of the way in which the new generation of workers who contribute to the global economy are best led and managed. Arguably, project team members on complex virtual teams fall into the category of knowledge worker for the reasons discussed below.

Knowledge workers are broadly defined as persons contributing to the knowledge economy (a post-industrial, post-service economic system). They are self-motivated, challenge-seeking persons who capture, manipulate and apply knowledge to create value. Knowledge workers usually know more about their job than their manager or anyone else in the organisation, and who often do not consider themselves to be subordinates in the traditional sense [32]. Knowledge workers cannot therefore be managed/lead in the same way as industrial or service workers.

One of Australia's leading academics, Professor Glyn Davis is recognised as an outstanding leader in a knowledge environment, having been described in those terms by former Queensland Premier Peter Beattie [32]. Professor Davis, who is currently (in 2012) the Vice Chancellor of Melbourne University, says that leaders should not tell knowledge workers what to do, but rather need to understand *what* they do and then lead by persuasive vision. This can be effected by:

- The views and visions of the knowledge workers are aggregated and shaped into a consistent theme,

- A vision based on these embedded values is developed,

- The vision thus formulated is articulated *back* to the knowledge workers with empathy and enthusiasm,

- The leader demonstrates high credibility,

- An understanding of the business and,

- Clear support for the business,

- The leader must be perceived as the embodiment of the values of the organisation,

- The leader skilfully uses multiple channels of communication to convey a consistent message that makes people feel good about working for the organisation. (This sounds similar to Eisenhower's idea of leadership being about *getting people to want to do what it is you want them to do*).

Skryme [33] outline some guidelines for the leadership of knowledge workers, distilled from the management literature. At a high-level, the critical leadership factors are a well articulated vision, a clear understanding of the link between knowledge and business benefits, together with effective marketing promotion. The leader must have a deep belief in the value of knowledge management to the organisation, and a commitment to innovative thinking and acting (including the willingness to commit resources).

DuBrin et al [32] summarise the leadership factors for knowledge workers as follows:

- Individual development plans for staff,

- Acquisition of innovative projects,

- Team composition; multi-disciplinary roles and mentoring/coaching,

- Use of quality systems,

- Systematic project evaluations,

- Planning for both formal and informal communications,

- Culture in which success and failure are discussed openly,

- Specific knowledge may become redundant but the ability to learn always remains valuable to the organisation,

- Knowledge workers' values must be aligned with those of the organisation,

Challenges of global software development

Holmstrom et al [34] discuss three kinds of distance in the arena of global software development – temporal, geographical, and socio-cultural – and present a useful view of how this distance dimension can relate to the software development process dimension. While this is not specifically about leadership, it can be argued that like the integrated teaming material from the CMMI-IPPD, these factors represent leadership challenges. An effective virtual team leader will find ways to address these issues effectively.

It can be seen also that there is overlap with the explicit leadership challenges outlined by Bell and Kozlowski [34].

Effective virtual team leadership

Zhang, Fjermestad and Tremaine [27] in their review of earlier virtual team leadership studies suggest that given the inconsistencies inherent in the results, that a 'contingency' approach to studying team leadership might be appropriate. Contingency in this context refers to there being no single set of leadership skills that bring about effective virtual team leadership; rather that effectiveness is contingent upon contextual variables and situational complexity.

The contextual variables identified [27] from their review of the literature include:

- **Communication media richness facilitating Trust.** The technology's ability to provide an environment that provides a rich perceptual experience for the participants. This includes immediate feedback, the number of perceptual cues and communication channels used, and the personalization of messages. Media richness facilitates trust between leadership and team member by minimising team process degradation while maximising motivation and commitment to a successful project outcome.

- **Goal-frustrating events managed by Optimism.** Obstacles and set-backs like technical problems, deadline pressures that threaten the accomplishment of the prescribed project objectives. This creates negative affect among team members, which can amplify itself over time to create a significant problem for the team. Inspirational motivation, optimism, individualized consideration and contingent reward all appear to optimise team performance by creating a positive affective climate.

- **Leader/follower gender, improved individualised consideration.** Female leaders have been shown to improve virtual team performance by exhibiting a higher degree of Individualized consideration behavior which causes higher levels of team satisfaction with the leadership. Combining individualized consideration with contingent reward further improves the leadership effectiveness of female virtual team leaders. In addition, in female-only groups, the effect of a charismatic virtual team leader is enhanced through effective trust-building.

Sloan Distributed Leadership Model

Ancona, Malone, Orlikowski and Senge [36] at the Sloan School of Management have developed a Distributed Leadership Model that offers an approach to understanding and practicing leadership.

The Sloan Model basically outlines four dimensions of leadership [36]:

Sense making -- the process of making sense of the world around us, understanding the context in which we are operating:

- Get data from multiple sources: customers, suppliers, employees, competitors, other departments, and investors.

- Involve others in your sense making. Say what you think you are seeing, and check with people who have different perspectives from yours.

- Use early observations to shape small experiments in order to test your conclusions. Look for new ways to articulate alternatives and better ways to understand options.

- Do not simply apply existing frameworks but instead be open to new possibilities. Try not to describe the world in stereotypical ways, such as good guys and bad guys, victims and oppressors, or marketers and engineers.

Relating -- developing strategic relationships within and across organizations:

- Spend time trying to understand others' perspectives, listening with an open mind and without judgment.

- Encourage others to voice their opinions. What do they care about? How do they interpret what's going on? Why?

- Before expressing your ideas, try to anticipate how others will react to them and how you might best explain them.

- When expressing your ideas, don't just give a bottom line; explain your reasoning process.

- Assess the strengths of your current connections: How well do you relate to others when receiving advice? When giving advice? When thinking through difficult problems? When asking for help?

Visioning-- creating a compelling and feasible vision of the future as it might apply to the organization

- Practice creating a vision in many arenas, including your work life, your home life, and in community groups. Ask yourself, 'What do I want to create?'

- Develop a vision about something that inspires you. Your enthusiasm will motivate you and others. Listen to what they find exciting and important.

- Expect that not all people will share your passion. Be prepared to explain why people should care about your vision and what can be achieved through it. If people don't get it, don't just turn up the volume. Try to construct a shared vision.

- Don't worry if you don't know how to accomplish the vision. If it is compelling and credible, other people will discover all sorts of ways to make it real –ways you never could have imagined on your own.

- Use images, metaphors, and stories to convey complex situations that will enable others to act.

Inventing – creating new ways of working together to realize the vision.

- Don't assume that the way things have always been done is the best way to do them.

- When a new task or change effort emerges, encourage creative ways of getting it done.

- Experiment with different ways of organizing work. Find alternative methods for grouping and linking people.

- When working to understand your current environment, ask yourself, 'What other options are possible?'

- All of the previous paragraphs derived from Ancona, Malone, Orlikowski and Senge, [36]

- The authors go on to describe the indications of when these activities are not being performed well:

Signs of weak sense making

- You feel strongly that you are usually right and others are often wrong.

- You feel your views describe reality correctly, but others' views do not.

- You find you are often blindsided by changes in your organization or industry.

- When things change, you typically feel resentful. (that's not the way it should be!)

Signs of weak relating

- You blame others for failed projects.

- You feel others are constantly letting you down or failing to live up to your expectations.

- You find that many of your interactions at work are unpleasant, frustrating, or argumentative.

- You find many of the people you work with untrustworthy.

Signs of weak visioning

- You feel your work involves managing an endless series of crises.

- You feel like you're bouncing from pillar to post with no sense of larger purpose.

- You often wonder, 'Why are we doing this?' or 'Does it really matter?'

- You can't remember the last time you talked to your family or a friend with excitement about your work.

Signs of weak inventing

- Your organization's vision seems abstract to you.

- You have difficulty relating your company's vision to what you are doing today.

- You notice dysfunctional gaps between your organization's aspirations and the way work is organized.

- You find that things tend to revert to business as usual.

- All of the previous paragraphs derived from Ancona, Malone, Orlikowski and Senge, [36].

References

[1] Bennis, W., Nanus, B., (1985) *Leaders: The strategies for taking charge*, Harper Row, New York.

[2] *New Oxford American Dictionary*, (2010) edited by Angus Stevenson and Christine A. Lindberg. Oxford University Press.

[3] Maslow, A. (1970) *Religion, Values and Peak Experiences*, Viking, New York.

[5] Takala, T., (1998). *Plato on Leadership*. Journal of Business Ethics 17: pp. 785-798

[6] Zaleznik, A., (2004*). Managers and Leaders: Are they different?*, Harvard Business Review, The Best of HBR edition, January. Article first published in 1977.

[7] Gemmill, G., Oakley, J., (1992). *Leadership: An alienating social myth?*, Human Relations, Vol. 45, Issue 2 pp. 113-129.

[8] Bennis W., Beiderman P. (1997). Organizing Genius: The Secrets of Creative Collaboration. Addison-Wesley.

[9] Bennis, W. (1994). On Becoming a Leader, *What Leaders Read 1*, Perseus Publishing, p 2.

[10] Bennis, W. (1999a). *The Leadership Advantage, Leader to Leader*, 12, p 12

[11] Bennis, W. (1999b), *Five Competencies of New Leaders, Executive Excellence*, 16 (7), pp.4-5.

[12] Offerman, L.R., Hanges, P.J. & Day, D.V. (2001). *Leaders, followers, and values; progress and prospects for theory and research, The Leadership Quarterly,* 12, pp. 129-131.

[13] Davis, T., Landa, M.J. (1999). *The Trust Deficit, Canadian Manager,* 21(1), pp. 10-27.

[14] Branham, L. (2005). The *7 Hidden Reasons Employees Leave,* American Management Association, 1st Edition, pp 19-20.

[15] Humphrey, W.S., (1997). *Managing Technical People: innovation, teamwork, and the software process.* Addison Wesley Longman, Reading Massachusetts.

[16] Champy, J. (2003), *The Hidden Qualities of Great Leaders, Fast Company Magazine,* 76, p 2.

[17] Macaluso, J. (2003). *Harnessing the Power of Emotional Intelligent Leadership,* The CEO Refresher, p 2.

[18] Zhang, S., Fjermestad, J., Tremaine, M., (2005). *Leadership Styles in Virtual Team Context: Limitations, Solutions and Propositions,* Proceedings of the 38th Hawaii International Conference on System Sciences.

[19] Bass, B., (1985). *Leadership and Performance beyond Expectations,* New York: The Free Press.

[20] Bass, B., Avolio, B. Goodheim, L., (1987). *Biography and the Assessment of Transformational Leadership at the World Class Level,* Journal of Management, vol. 13, pp. 7-19.

[21] Lowe, K., Kroeck K., Sivasubramaniam, N, (1996). *Effectiveness Correlates of Transformational and Transactional Leadership: a Meta-analytic Review of the MLQ Literature,* Leadership Quarterly, vol. 7, pp. 385-425.

[22] Bass, B, (1990). *Bass and Stodgill's Handbook of Leadership,* New York: Free Press.

[23] Bass, B., Avolio, B., (1993). *Transformational Leadership: A response to Critiques,* in M. M. Chemers & R. Ayman (Eds.), Leadership theory and research: Perspectives and directions, pp. 49-80, San Diego, CA: Academic Press.

[24] Kahai, S., Sosik, J. and Avolio, B. (1997). *Effects of Leadership Style and Problem Structure on Work Group Process and Outcomes in an Electronic Meeting System Environment,* Personnel Psychology, vol. 50, pp. 1-146.

[25] George, J., Easton, G. Jr., Nunamaker, J., and Northcraft, G., (1990). *A Study of Collaborative Work with and without Computer-based Support,* Information Systems Research, vol. 1, pp. 394-415.

[26] Lim, L., Raman, K., Wei, K., (1994). *Interacting Effects of GSS and Leadership,* Decision Support System, vol. 12, pp. 199-1.

[27] Avolio, B., Kahai, S., George, E., (2000). *E-leadership: Implications for Theory, Research, and Practice,* Leadership Quarterly, vol. 11, pp.615-668.

[28] McColl-Kennedy, J., Anderson, R., (2002*). Subordinate manager Gender Combination and Perceived Leadership Style Influence on Emotions, Self-esteem and Organizational Commitment,* Journal of Business Research, vol. 13, pp 545- 559.

[29] O'Leary, M., Orlikowski, W. J., & Yates, J. (2002). *Distributed work over the centuries: Trust and control in the Hudson's Bay Company, 1670–1826.* In P. Hinds & S.

Kiesler (Eds.), Distributed Work: 27–54. Cambridge, MA: MIT Press.

[30] Ahuja, M. K., Carley, K., & Galletta, D. F. (1997). *Individual performance in distributed design groups: An empirical study.* Paper presented at the SIGCPR Conference, San Francisco. p 165.

[31] Cascio, W., Shurygailo, S., (2003). *E-Leadership and Virtual Teams, Organizational Dynamics,* vol. 31, pp. 362-376.

[32] DuBrin, A., Dalglish, C., Miller, P (2006). *Leadership,* John Wiley, Australia, 2nd Edition, Brisbane.

[33] Skryme, D., (1998). *Measuring the Value of Knowledge,* Business Intelligence Limited, Wimbledon, United Kingdom.

[34] Bell, B.S., Kozlowski, S.W. (2002). *A Typology of Virtual Teams: Implications for Effective Leadership.* Group and Organisational Management, Vol. 27, No.1 pp. 14-19.

[35] Holmstrom, H., Fitzgerald, B., Agerfalk, P., Conchuir, E., (2006). *Agile Practices Reduce Distance in Global Software Development.* Information Systems Management; Summer 200623;3, p 9.

[36] Ancona, D., Malone, T., Orlikowski, W., Senge, P. (2007). *In Praise of the Incomplete Leader,* Harvard Business Review; Feb2007, Vol. 85 Issue 2, pp. 92-100.

Appendix: Rhetorical devices

Allusion - a reference to a work of literature, person, place, event, that is assumed to be sufficiently well known to be recognized by the reader as authoritative.

Anecdote - an entertaining story that illustrates a point, often biographical.

Aphorism - a concisely expressed statement of principle.

Appeal to authority – quoting someone recognized as an authority in a subject area in support of your argument.

Appeal to fear - an emotional appeal intended to arouse the audience's emotions in support of an argument.

Appeal to patriotism - an emotional appeal to a person's love of country, implying that if they disagree they are unpatriotic.

Appeal to pride - an emotional appeal aimed at convincing an they must act in order to maintain their dignity.

Anticipation of objection – pointing out the error in someone's objections before they say it.

Bandwagon - strengthening an argument by encouraging people to make the popular choice.

Conceit - an extended comparison of two different things.

Contrast - to point out striking differences.

Correction of erroneous views - indicating where your opponent's views are incorrect.

Concession - an acknowledgment of objections.

Corrective measures - proposing ways to eliminate undesirable conditions.

Emotional words – using language that stimulates strong emotions in the audience (essential with Charisma).

Extended metaphor - a long, drawn-out metaphor that makes a series of parallel comparisons (see conceit).

Holy War - an attempt to persuade the audience that God is on the side of the speaker. To disagree is to anger God.

Hyperbole – a gross exaggeration of the facts.

Imagery – vivid descriptions that impress images on the mind.

Irony – humorous or sarcastic expressions in which the real meaning of the words is the opposite of their usual meaning (see sarcasm).

Logical reasoning – adhering to the principles of correct reasoning.

Metonymy - using a part to name the whole, or using the name of one thing for that of another associated with it. e.g. referring to the President as "The White House"

Repetition - repeating words or phrases for emphasis.

Rhetorical question - asking a question to engage the audience without them needing to actually respond.